COPING™

COPING WHEN

A PARENT IS INCARCERATED

Carolyn DeCarlo

Rosen
YA™

New York

Published in 2019 by The Rosen Publishing Group, Inc.
29 East 21st Street, New York, NY 10010

Copyright © 2019 by The Rosen Publishing Group, Inc.

First Edition

Expert Reviewer: Heather Gay, LCSW

Library of Congress Cataloging-in-Publication Data

Names: DeCarlo, Carolyn, author.
Title: Coping when a parent is incarcerated / Carolyn DeCarlo.
Description: New York : Rosen Publishing, 2019. | Series: Coping | Includes bibliographical references and index. | Audience: Grades 7–12.
Identifiers: LCCN 2017051478| ISBN 9781508178996 (library bound) | ISBN 9781508178989 (pbk.)
Subjects: LCSH: Children of prisoners—United States—Juvenile literature. | Prisoners—Family relationships—United States—Juvenile literature. | Families—United States—Juvenile literature.
Classification: LCC HV8886.U5 D43 2019 | DDC 362.82/9508350973—dc23
LC record available at https://lccn.loc.gov/2017051478

Manufactured in the United States of America

CONTENTS

INTRODUCTION

What if you were only allowed to spend four weekends a year at your father's place? For many teenagers, this would be a drastic reduction in the amount of time they would normally spend together. But for others, this might come as a treat. For Sylvia Harvey, growing up with an incarcerated parent meant she visited her dad at least four times a year on the grounds of Soledad State Prison, in a fully furnished apartment, as part of the California Department of Corrections' family visiting program.

Most of the year, Sylvia lived with her grandmother—a familiar situation, because her mother had died when she was three and her father began serving sixteen years to life when she was just five. But

It is important for parents and babies to spend time bonding. From the start, children need their parents or guardians as teachers, caregivers, and models for development.

5

Sylvia didn't feel distant from her father growing up; beyond looking forward to "big breakfasts" (clanging pots, hash browns in the skillet, eggs, and biscuits) with her father and four older brothers on these special weekends, they stayed connected through phone calls, weekly letters, and pictures. These links were important to Sylvia. Although her dad was in prison, Sylvia was able to grow up with a positive relationship with him. "Those weekends rate as some of the best moments of my childhood," Sylvia recalls.

Unfortunately, Sylvia's access to those visits with her dad was eliminated by the state of California in 1996, when she was fifteen, as progressive policies shut down in the face of prison overcrowding and budget cuts. In fact, only four states still retain special programs such as the one from which Sylvia and her family benefited.

Things are so different now. You are probably shocked to learn that policies like this one could ever have been in place in the United States—let alone, common practice. But long ago, for some American teens just like you, it was a reality. Once, nine states allowed them. In Mississippi, a similar setup (loosely based on the idea of the conjugal visit, which was rolled out in the state almost a century before) only folded in 2014.

Not all relationships with incarcerated parents are positive, nor could they all be saved through increased visitation rights or miniholidays with the imprisoned parent. But for many in Sylvia's position, finding some way to establish common ground and an open line of communication with that parent can be paramount to maintaining a healthy connection between those individuals. There are many styles of family dynamics to consider and many situations where extended visits would not be a good solution, but that is part of what we're here to discover.

You'll be learning more about the state of parental incarceration in the United States both historically and today, giving you the tools to seek both personal coping strategies and public policy changes that would benefit our society as a whole. Trauma is devastating, and it touches so many young people whose lives have been uprooted by the prison system. In this resource, you will not only learn how to heal from the trauma you've experienced as a result but also how to put practical steps in place to reduce or even eliminate it from your future.

CHAPTER ONE

Defining the Issue

Based on Sylvia Harvey's example—or, potentially, if life with an incarcerated parent has always been your status quo—you may be wondering, what could be so bad about it? To be sure, there are plenty of other reasons why a child could find himself or herself separated from a living parent in the United States, such as from divorce, the nature of a parent's job, custody rights, social services, immigration, and so on. Why even focus at all on this one type of relationship and its origin? Why not just discuss them together, as they all boil down to a child growing up without consistent access to one or both parents?

Not all separations are dramatic or traumatic, and of course this applies both to children with incarcerated parents and in general. However, there are some very important facts to explain when focusing on the effects of parental

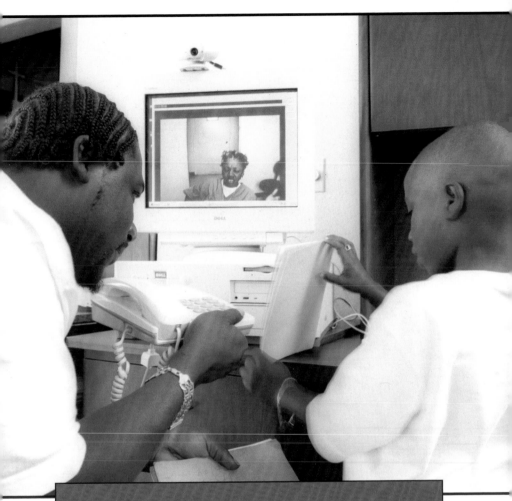

Some prisons are exploring alternative ways for inmates and their loved ones to conduct visits, such as this "virtual video" program run by the Florida Department of Corrections.

incarceration on young people, and these statistics and truths are individual to cases involving imprisonment of the parent. If you are one of these people, hopefully these facts will help remind you that you are not alone and give you some strength to fight for positive change.

Just being the child of an incarcerated parent increases one's own chances for incarceration. It is important to stop this cycle by uncovering the causes for trauma before there are effects.

Acting Out

For many, a parent's incarceration can have a lasting negative impact on the child's mental and physical health, leading to both behavioral issues and below-average academic performance. Though Child Trends researchers admit to some uncertainty surrounding long-term impact studies because of a lack of existing research in this field, data has exposed a disturbing assortment of adverse childhood experiences (ACEs)—in other words, more immediately identifiable negative outcomes that appear when the child is still a child (or a teen). According to Cooper and Murphey, these immediate outcomes include "increased risk for trauma, or toxic stress, particularly ... cumulative."

Greater than 50 percent of children experiencing parental incarceration had at one point been living with someone with a substance-abuse problem, as compared with less than 10 percent of children without a parent in jail. Almost three in five had also had parents who were divorced or separated, compared with one in five outside the prison system. More than one-third had observed violence between their parents or caretakers, and another third had observed or faced violence locally, such as in their communities. As a quick comparison, fewer than one-tenth of those who did not have an incarcerated parent had experienced violence at home or in their communities. Finally,

Contact visits are vital because they provide just that: physical contact between parent and child. For that brief time, the parent and child interact face to face, even permitting a brief hug.

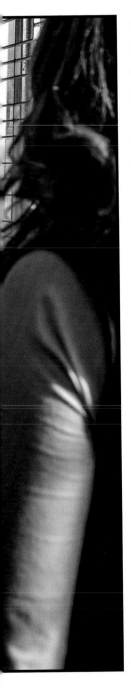

more than one out of four children had resided with someone who was mentally ill or suicidal, and nearly one out of ten had endured a parent's death.

Potential long-term negative effects would likely increase young people's vulnerability for fallout from the loss of a so-called attachment figure (the incarcerated parent), leading to a toxic cycle of crisis that (according to statistics) often ends in the child's own incarceration as an adult. So, what can be done to remove these adverse childhood experiences from the mix altogether? How can we stop the immediate problems, therefore removing the possibilities for long-term negative effects as well? There is a need for effective programming, primarily from within the prisons themselves, to mitigate future harm.

Contact Visits

While the look and feel of prison visitation differs between one state and another (as well as between prisons), most visits, known as contact visits, occur in a controlled setting, with tables, chairs, vending machines, and (occasionally) games designed to keep the inmates and their guests entertained. These visits are heavily guarded and permit only brief physical contact: when arriving and departing a hug and kiss are allowed but must last fewer than fifteen seconds.

To get in—and get there—families have to travel on average 100 miles (161 kilometers), undergoing metal detector tests and long wait times, all for a short visit that allows for very little stimulation or freedom of imagination. In some places, these visits are allowed only monthly; in others, more frequent visits may be on offer, but in reality, families are restricted by personal limitations, such as access to transportation, accommodation, or another parent or guardian's work schedule.

The Origin of the Contact Visit

The ordinary contact visit still in operation today can trace its roots to a very different kind of visitation: the conjugal visit. A plan first introduced into the Mississippi State Penitentiary in 1918 for African American inmates, the visits were extended to white men in the 1930s and women by 1972. In 1963, the prison added a marriage requirement. The only inmates who were qualified to participate were on the minimum or medium security level and exhibited good behavior; they were also pretested for infectious diseases. Done appropriately, the purpose of the conjugal visit was to give inmates the opportunity to confirm the well-being of their families and strengthen their ties despite so many boundaries.

In 1974, Mississippi took its program a step further, launching a family visitation program. This type of visit welcomed parents, siblings, and children, as well as spouses. As a tool for rehabilitation, the family visitation program made use of local support to provide small, furnished apartments for visits lasting from three to five days. Several other states followed Mississippi's lead, including California, South Carolina, New York, Minnesota, Washington, Connecticut, New Mexico, and Wyoming.

However, the focus on keeping families together even when one of the parents was incarcerated began to wane in the 1990s, with the passage of President Bill Clinton's Violent Crime Control and Law Enforcement Act in 1994. It put into place obligatory minimum sentencing enhancements, expanded death penalty use, and restricted prisoners' access to facilities and other

(continued on the next page)

(continued from the previous page)

services, such as continuing education. A No Frills Prison Act followed it the next year, which was aimed at removing prison "frills" such as exercise machines and hot plates. The first of the conjugal and extended-family visiting programs to go were in South Carolina and Wyoming, with tougher requirements cropping up almost everywhere else and changing times and conditions cited for the restrictions. In 2012, Mississippi ended its options for extended-family visits, followed by conjugal visits in 2014; today, very few examples remain intact from these freer days.

The Phillips family represents a typical example of the strain that maintaining regular contact visits can have on a family, as well as being a uniquely historic representation of the institution of the family visitation program in Mississippi. Until September 2012, Victoria Phillips and her two daughters—both of whom were lawfully conceived within the grounds of the penitentiary by way of the program—were able to visit their respective spouse and father for three to five days in a small apartment on the facility. For six years, Victoria and her incarcerated husband felt as though they were able to raise a family together, with memories of barbecuing, basketball, and bedtime stories.

This freedom ended when the program was removed in 2012, but the family has kept up with monthly contact visits supplemented with regular phone calls. The contact visits are admittedly better than nothing, but they lack the diversity of stimuli the family visitation program had to offer. Though Victoria does her best to maintain a positive relationship between her incarcerated husband and two young children, she struggles to make the monthly trek to the penitentiary and is frustrated by the lack of materials, games, and freedom that formerly made bonding so much easier for the foursome.

Former Mississippi corrections commissioner Christopher Epps described his reasons for cutting the program in a press release. He said that the budget could not handle the costs involved in tasks such as taking care of the building and moving inmates to and from the visiting space, explaining that he felt "the benefits of the programs don't outweigh the cost."

Direct Intervention

As it stands today, incarcerated parents are more likely to have experienced the benefits of effective

Some prisons are able to offer classes for inmates across a wide variety of topics, including practical ones such as parenting.

programming than their children. In-prison programs that place a primary focus on parenting skills have actually been quite common—which is great. The problem here is that by comparison, precious few of these prison-driven programs actually give equal attention to the needs of the children. This is where the focus must be shifted toward helping incarcerated individuals and their children form positive connections—and keeping them connected in positive ways over the months or years spent apart.

The method of direct intervention is generally seen as most useful in helping to connect incarcerated parents—and then keep them connected—with their children. These programs should focus diversely on families, schools, and neighborhoods (including awareness training for communities and educators), with an aim to decrease the shame and stigma that parents and children alike may feel toward the incarcerated individual and his or her position in society. If the link between a parent and his or her child can be maintained or even strengthened while he or she is serving the sentence, it will be substantially harder for that ever-unproductive shame to wiggle its way in.

It is important to involve the support of the community before reintegration has even begun, rather than waiting to rehabilitate incarcerated parents once they have left the prison system and reentered society. As early as sentencing, the prison system needs to provide more guidance for families of offenders, in order for them to maintain or even regain a familial bond. Maintaining a link with a parent in prison is of paramount importance to the child. Not only should it be easier for prisoners to spend time with loved ones but both the child and parent need to feel safe in this environment. If a prison provides a contact visit, the prison must be held accountable for the quality of the time spent visiting. Similarly, prisons need to engage with communities to help; rehabilitation and inclusion of families is incredibly important at the time of reintegration, but it also needs to be available to families throughout the parent's period of incarceration.

Additionally, normalization of the situation is key to removing stigma for both parties. If the parent and child feel supported by a system that integrates their situation with the community and society right from the beginning, there are fewer opportunities

When you are a child, anything that sets you apart from your peers can be fodder for gossip, including having a parent in the prison system.

for shame to take root. Because of a variety of reasons, including both fictional portrayals of life in prison and statistics hyped in the news media, and housing stipulations and laws, some communities and neighborhoods have been typically wary of accepting former inmates and families of current inmates back into their folds. Children are bullied by their peers; parents are questioned both for their ability to raise their children alone and for their decision to maintain or break from their relationship with the incarcerated person; and the incarcerated parent is questioned even more extensively on the outcomes of their actions, not least of which is their possible danger to the community or their own family. When the system intervenes even just to educate schools and the communities involved, stigma and shame may be reduced.

Community-Based Child Support

Related to the issue of a lack of opportunities from the community is the stark reality that for many families living within limited economic means, options for child support can be scarce. This tends to have a more dramatic affect on black and Latino families in the prison system. A 2010 survey conducted by the government found that fifty-one thousand federal prisoners had child support orders, with almost twenty-nine thousand of them behind on payments.

In America, incarcerated persons are expected to pay a portion of their child support while in prison. However, the Obama administration issued new rules in 2016 to lessen this burden, aimed toward relieving inmates struggling to repay debts upon release, which can lead to recidivism, or the committing of another crime, sometimes repeatedly. The hope is that by making the child support payments more attainable, it will result in more reliable payments—ultimately helping not only prisoners' return to society but their children over the short and long term.

Although this type of government intervention has clear potential benefits for both incarcerated persons and their families, the question remains: Who will help the families and children on the outside, and whose households do not meet the requirement of $24,000 from owed child support? Kinship care—or caretaking undergone by nontraditional guardians—can be both a blessing and a burden on the children of incarcerated persons. When one parent is imprisoned and the other parent is deemed in some way unfit to raise their child himself or herself (or at all), this responsibility falls first to other family members and then to the community or society in general. In the urban African American community, this generally implicates the maternal grandmother.

Though grandparents (and other kin) can provide fantastic support systems for young people,

Most grandparents would do anything to provide loving support for their grandchildren while their parents are incarcerated, but they may not always be their most suitable caregivers.

the reality for many—especially those living in urban, poor areas affected by crime and incarceration— involves an amount of difficulty and complexity. A degree of responsibility here lies with the child welfare agencies in determining the capability of the family member to care for the child. Although keeping the family together is generally considered preferable, grandparents who have become caregivers may feel that it is a burden, especially if they already try to make ends meet on a limited income or with little or no help or backing from social services. Particularly when the mother is incarcerated, child care relies upon the grandmother. Studies have shown that the rate of female incarceration has increased by 11 percent per year since 1985, with a disproportionately higher number of women of color. Add to that the fact that more than 50 percent of children whose mothers are incarcerated are cared for by their grandmothers, you can easily understand the need for social intervention.

Myths & FACTS

Myth: It is unusual for mothers to be given jail time and therefore unlikely for your mother or a classmate's mother to be incarcerated.

Fact: According to the Sentencing Project, incarceration rates for women in the United States have risen by 700 percent from 1980 to 2014. This growth rate even outpaces men by 50 percent. State prisons are filled with about two-thirds of women who are there serving time for nonviolent offenses, with the trend of mass incarceration potentially still on the rise (if Attorney General Jeff Sessions has anything to say about it). In fact, women are far more likely to be primary caregivers, and in American state prisons, 60 percent of women's children are younger than age eighteen.

Myth: Incarcerated people are unfit to be parents.

Fact: Today's average prisoner may not look or act the way you'd expect. According to studies done by the Justice Program at the Brennan Center for Justice at the

NYU School of Law, of the current 2.2 million people in prison, 39 percent of the nationwide prison population shouldn't be behind bars and were sent there with little public safety rationale. One-quarter of prisoners (that's 364,000 people, as of 2016) are nonviolent, low-level offenders who would get far more benefit from treatment, community service, or probation. If these people are not dangerous and would benefit more from being out of prison than on the inside, it is also unfair to class them as unfit for parenting.

Myth: All children of incarcerated parents are more apt to commit crimes themselves and are generally low achievers and caught up in the prison system.

Fact: Steve Christian pointed out to the National Conference of State Legislatures in 2009 that there is no empirical, or firsthand, data to support the claim that those children with parents who are incarcerated are six times more liable to grow up into adults who are incarcerated, too. Although those in the field agree that children of incarcerated

(*continued on the next page*)

27

Many people assume that celebrities have always lived charmed lives, but that is not the case for Leighton Meester (*Gossip Girl*). Meester's mother was incarcerated while pregnant with her.

(*continued from the previous page*)

adults find themselves vulnerable to a host of risks, and their lives may be an uphill battle, it has yet to be established that there is a contributory connection between an adult's incarceration and his or her child's difficulties.

Alternatively, there are many successful individuals whose parents were incarcerated. Actor Woody Harrelson's father spent most of his life in prison after being convicted on two murder charges. Drew Barrymore's father went to jail several times in the 1950s and 1960s for public drunkenness, drug abuse, and domestic violence. *Gossip Girl* actress Leighton Meester's mother, Constance, was serving time in federal prison while pregnant with Meester, after having been convicted as part of a drug ring that smuggled marijuana from Jamaica to the United States. Meester's grandparents raised her until her mother was released from prison. American soccer goalkeeper Hope Solo was conceived during a conjugal visit while her father, Jeffrey, was in prison for embezzlement.

CHAPTER TWO

Prevalence in Society

No matter who you are, there has probably been a point in your life where you have felt like you were all alone—whether studying for an impossible test, improving your sprint time by that last tenth of a second, or memorizing lines for the community play. But then you went to your classroom, turned up at the track meet, or walked onto the stage and found yourself surrounded by a group of other people all with the same goal, all having experienced the same struggle as you. Sure, some of them may not have studied as hard or might have a naturally longer stride, but essentially, you discover, these people are in it with you.

Many children may not need to be reminded that their family is normal or that their home life is common to many others around them in society. In fact, as it turns out many things that would not have been seen as "normal" family dynamics several decades ago have since increased in visibility, if not commonality.

The American Psychological Association (APA) reports that 40 to 50 percent of US marriages will end in divorce. In 2015, a Gallup poll calculated that 780,000 Americans are married to a same-sex partner and an additional two million reside with a same-sex domestic partner. In all likelihood, that number will rise in the future, because in 2015 the Supreme Court decided to abolish all remaining bans on same-sex marriage. If, according to the US Census Bureau in 2016, 69 percent of the 73.7 million US children younger than age eighteen live with families that have two parents, this would suggest that a significant 31 percent do not. In fact, according to the US Census Bureau again, there are about twelve million single-parent families in 2016, while one in four children younger than the age of eighteen—about 17.2 million—are being raised without a father, and almost half are living below the poverty line.

Facts and Figures

So you may be thinking, these facts and figures are all great, but what do they have to do with me? My parents aren't divorced, but they are both incarcerated. My mother isn't a lesbian, but she's serving five years in prison. And I am here all alone because my friends'

It is common for children of incarcerated parents to feel alone and even unwanted, but you may be surprised to learn just how common your circumstances really are.

parents aren't in jail, and I am teased about it by my classmates nearly every day. Well, first, your school may be exceptional, because the number of Americans in federal and state prisons and jails has quintupled over the past four decades, which is more than six times the average across developed nations. So, the fact that several—if not many, as is the case for some communities—of your other classmates have not seen a parent serve jail time is phenomenal.

According to the Justice Department, for every two US prisoners released, one returns home to a minor child. Additionally, one in fourteen American children has experienced life with a parent in jail, and more than five million children in the United States (roughly 7 percent) have seen a parent who lived with them go to jail. These findings were echoed in a 2015 study by the Center for American Progress (CAP), which discovered that between 33 and 36.5 million children, or almost half the total population of children in the

United States, have at least one parent with a criminal record. So, how is it possible that something so common could ever be seen as isolating? How could something that almost half of the American population under the age of eighteen is dealing with be seen as unusual, let alone cause for stigma or shame?

Part of the answer lies in its newness as a phenomenon. In 2010, the Pew Charitable Trusts reported a sharp increase in jail and prison populations: they found 2.3 million people were currently in jail or prison in that year, which means one in twenty-eight American children (3.6 percent, or 2.7 million minor children) currently have an incarcerated parent, as compared with twenty-five years before, in 1985, when the number was one in 125. Again, this can be attributed to the concept of mass incarceration, evoking a period of time in US history during which the number of offenders being given significant prison sentences for primarily nonviolent crimes spiked in an effort to crack down on drug-related offenses. Prison was used as punishment for drug offenses and other nonaggressive charges, which may previously have had less fearsome results, such as probation, fines, or community service.

Another factor is race. Incarceration in the United States disproportionately affects black families. According to Child Trends, one in nine black children have had a parent in prison. A black child is twice as likely to have a parent behind bars, with nearly 14 percent of all black youths between twelve and seventeen (in 2015) having seen a parent go to jail during their lifetime. This could, in fact, even be an underestimation, as it this statistic does not account for parents who do not live with their children. Not only are black children disproportionately represented in the prison system, but poor children and children whose parents have had less education are also more likely to be affected. Children in poor families are three times more likely to have a parent in prison than high-income households. Sadly, the vast majority of incarcerated parents across all groups are fathers.

Mothers and Daughters

Approximately 7 percent of Mississippi's prisoners are women. Cristina Pierre was once among those women as well as a part of the family visitation program unique to that state. She and her daughters were allowed the (occasional, sanctioned) time and freedom to bond in a family house. Pierre says the structure of the family house gave her the chance to be a mother and comforted her oldest daughter, Briana. "You can't hug on them like you would want

(continued on the next page)

(continued from the previous page)

to. And you really just can't talk, because you got everybody in your business," she says, comparatively, of the general contact visit. Upon incarceration, Pierre lost custody of all but one of her five children, but the two credit the family house for their lasting bond. "She would probably not know me," Pierre imagines of Briana. "When you have that big of a space between you and your children for all them years, they do forget, if they're young... my other children have no clue who I am."

They lost access to the family house in 2012 but have worked things out pretty well. But few female prisoners have had the same access to initiatives like the one in Mississippi. Oklahoma inmate Janay Manning reveals that her teen daughter is disappointed in her. Manning, a nonviolent drug offender, is handcuffed to the wall during her interview. Although the number of male inmates is finally starting to decline post-mass incarceration, two-thirds of the women in state prisons are there for nonviolent offenses. Although society often feels fear and contempt for felons, in reality these mothers are rarely a danger; with rehabilitation programs available instead of or even after serving prison time, these women could get back to being mothers and more productive members of society.

Why Now?

The United States currently has the most people incarcerated of any other country in the so-called developed world. More generally, across the country, more than two million people are presently incarcerated (in jails and prisons), most of who are blacks and Latinos. Compared to white men, black men are six times more likely and Latino men are 2.5 times more likely to be incarcerated. And to reiterate, for every two prisoners currently being released, one is returning home to at least one minor child. This means there is an incredibly significant number of children in the United States living with a parent in prison or in jail—and not all that many resources are being used to provide help for these families, let alone empower them or bring about any future change.

So, why is this so topical? First, two big reports from Child Trends and the Center for American Progress came out in 2015 that both made a strong case for bringing issues faced by incarcerated people with children and families into the center ring when discussing criminal justice. Evolving legislative and policy changes in the 2010s have also driven advocates to speak up on these issues. And while there has been plenty of analysis on financial costs to communities, cities, and states (which, unsurprisingly, have all dramatically increased since the 1980s), there has been no equivalent meaningful law addressing the socioeconomic standing of present or past prisoners and their families except for the Second Chance Act.

The Second Chance Act was a bill introduced in 2007 under President George W. Bush and ushered into law in 2008 by then senator Joe Biden and Representative Danny K. Davis, allowing aging prisoners to transfer to home confinement and receive reentry grants, or a sum of money upon re-entering society. Receiving bipartisan support, the Second Chance Act was allocated around $65 million for distribution to both state and local governments through grants over a period of two years. The purpose of the act is to:

- Support constructive rehabilitation of formerly incarcerated individuals upon their return to society
- Give employment opportunities, drug and alcohol abuse treatment, shelter, family services, victim support, and other forms of aid to improve reintegration
- Offer mentoring to all offenders, including juveniles
- Provide family-based therapy for incarcerated persons with children under the age of eighteen
- Extend guidance to the Bureau of Prisons for improving steps toward the release of inmates
- Deliver information to the recently incarcerated regarding maintenance of health, personal

Receiving bipartisan support for its reforms for prisoners and the formerly convicted, President George W. Bush signed the Second Chance Act into law in 2008.

finance, and gainful employment; use of community resources; and avoiding recidivism.

While beneficiaries of the act include families and children of incarcerated persons, the act is also meant to help tackle the more general issues of substance abuse, mental health issues, undereducation, poor job skills, and high rates of reincarceration amongst offenders. Additionally, the National Reentry Resource Center was created by the Second Chance Act to collect, organize, and share information with interested organizations and assistance providers.

According to studies, between seventy and one hundred million Americans (or, one in three adults) have a criminal record of some kind. Even just a minor record can present obstacles for employment, housing, education and training, public assistance, and financial empowerment. In addition, there are some intergenerational consequences stemming from the possession of a criminal record, with identifiable—but not insurmountable—barriers to opportunities. An update called the Second Chance Reauthorization Act, introduced by US representatives Jim Sensenbrenner and Danny K. Davis, would renew this bipartisan piece of legislation for an additional four years, expanding the number of grants available and including increased attention to family needs, with children as a particular focus according to sponsor and Republican senator

Ohio senator Rob Portman sponsored the renewal of the
Second Chance Act (as the Second Chance Reauthorization Act),
increasing attention for families affected by the prison system.

Rob Portman of Ohio. This is important because it's currently estimated that 95 percent of those in prison will eventually go back to being a part of society. "It is in all of our interests to give these individuals a second chance," say Portman and Davis.

Social Welfare

In 2013, the Department of Health and Human Services' Administration for Children and Families created the Children of Incarcerated Parents' Working Group, led by the White House Domestic Policy Council, which includes representatives from the Department of Health and Human Services and also the Department of Justice, the Department of Housing and Urban Development, the Department of Agriculture, the Department of Education, and the Social Security Administration. This working group produced a tool kit geared toward finding solutions, which was then circulated among prison bureaus, welfare agencies, and residential reentry centers. Madeleine Solan, a social science analyst with the Department of Health and Human Services, is the cochair with the Department of Justice of the interagency working group. She says the real focus of the group is on supporting children of incarcerated parents, who are "an invisible group with a number of different struggles... our group tries to support them through thinking" in solutions-oriented ways to keep up their resilience during a "difficult period of having their parent either in state or federal prison or in jail."

But why focus on these children now? And why develop a tool kit designed for the prisons, welfare industries, and residential reentry centers—rather than the children themselves? Not only did the Child Trends study find that children with a residential parent

When your parent is incarcerated, it may feel like the odds are stacked against you. Statistically, you're likely to experience many adverse childhood experiences, but don't give up hope!

(meaning, a parent they lived with in the same home environment prior to the parent's incarceration) are also more likely to experience frequent social and economic hardship, parental divorce or separation, witnessing domestic violence in the household, or witnessing neighborhood violence, they found that for all of these adverse childhood experiences (ACEs), children who'd had a parent in the prison system had, on average, 1.4 more adverse childhood experiences than those who'd never had a residential incarcerated parent.

As for the second half of the question, another set of barriers appears for consideration—mostly to do with communication and change within the system itself. Incarcerated parents may be transferred from one prison facility to another fairly abruptly, making it difficult for social workers to keep up with their whereabouts, let alone mail and other pamphlets, or even their own children! Communication barriers (from difficulty receiving phone calls, to prison rules, to language barriers) also contribute. So an effective way around these communication barriers has been to put the tool kits directly into the system and let the children, parents, social workers, and prison guards access them there.

Personal Coping Strategies

Your friend Jessica asks you to come over for a girls' night on Saturday, but you have to say no. It's not that you don't want to, but you'll be taking care of your little brother, who is still too young to be left alone at night, while your mom finishes up her evening shift at the hospital where she works as a nurse. By the time she gets home, she will be exhausted but will probably spend a few hours at the kitchen table "upcycling" clothes for the consignment shop down the road where she's able to pick up a bit of extra cash every week. You wait to do the washing until she's home so she can quiz you on your vocabulary words for the test in English class on Monday.

In school on Monday, the test goes all right but you're distracted by Becky, who won't stop

You may be asked to babysit your siblings when all you want to do is spend time with your friends. Try to be nice—remember what it felt like to be their age?

kicking the back of your chair. "We were all talking about you at Jessica's party on Saturday," she starts in, "Where were you?" You keep your focus on the paper in front of you. "Altercation," she whispers one of the vocabulary words at you. "Your father knows all about those, doesn't he?" Your face flushes red, but you keep answering the test questions. "Destitute," she says a little louder, picking at a hole in your favorite sweater. "Girls whose fathers go to prison end up destitute."

You wouldn't need to have an incarcerated parent to feel a sense of familiarity with that situation. Teen bullies—and sometimes even well-meaning friends—can be insensitive at their best, purposefully abusive at their worst. It is unclear what Becky's intentions are, but studies have shown that when children of incarcerated parents are teased at school, this leads directly to lower self-esteem, anger, defiance, and desire for retaliation.

Looking Inward

People don't always have the easiest time confronting their own feelings. It can be easier to tuck them away inside, or even lash out physically, than sit in contemplation. But sometimes it is important to reveal one's own feelings—to a friend, a mentor, or a counselor—to find ways of dealing with what might feel like an overwhelming problem. Sometimes just finding someone to listen or say "me, too" can help.

According to a study conducted by the Urban Institute Justice Policy Center, children experience a set of common feelings when a parent is incarcerated based on their age group:

- Ages two to six: "Separation anxiety, impaired socio-emotional development, traumatic stress, survivor guilt"

47

Are you having trouble getting out of bed in the morning? Chronic sleeplessness, difficulty concentrating, and depression are all known effects of having a parent in prison.

- Ages seven to ten: "Developmental regressions, poor self-concept, acute traumatic stress reactions, impaired ability to overcome future trauma"
- Ages eleven to fourteen: "Rejection on limits of behavior and trauma-reactive behaviors"
- Ages fifteen to eighteen: "Premature termination of dependency relationship with parent, leading to potential for intergenerational crime/incarceration"

This study found that while younger children primarily experience disorganized feelings and behaviors, older children are more likely to display antisocial behavior, conduct disorders, and depression. Other emotional issues they face include chronic sleeplessness, difficulty concentrating, and temporary school phobias, which can often disrupt attendance.

It is important to confront these feelings and behaviors when the child is young to keep stress, anxiety, and guilt from building up with nowhere to go and no healthy outlet. It is also important to note that while some of these feelings may develop at a very early age, it is not at all uncommon to keep feeling them as a teenager, especially if left unspoken or unaddressed, in conjunction with latent reactions such as more physically reactive behavior. There is no single cure-all for the stew of negative thoughts you've got simmering, but there are some commonly suggested

One way to relieve stress at home or school is by taking time to write down your thoughts. If you find yourself with a quiet moment, seize it.

ways of coping with them, not least of which is one that has been discussed a bit in the previous text: talking it out. But there are other options, too, if talking is not your thing, such as journaling or free writing, where you might just sit down and start moving your pen on the page; going for a walk; or engaging in a more visually creative approach such as drawing or painting. You can also write a more pointed letter to a parent, friend, or peer. (The decision to post that letter—or destroy it!—is then completely up to you.)

A recent national study conducted by Child Welfare Services for recently arrested parents showed that one in five children presented with internalizing issues, including depression, anxiety, and withdrawal, whereas one in ten children exhibited externalizing problems, such as aggression, attention problems, and disruptive behavior. It is important to try to deal with internal issues before they develop into physical reactions, particularly those that harm you or those around you. But at the end of the day, this is all an attempt to avoid the early loss of a child's relationship with a parent, incarcerated or not, which can lead to a higher potential for intergenerational crime and incarceration.

A Healthy Life

Keshawn Green, age twenty, was conceived in prison. His father is thirty-four years into a life sentence, which in Mississippi means he won't ever get out. He has spent a long time thinking about

(continued on the next page)

(continued from the previous page)

what this background means for him and how he feels about the prison system. He suspects the corrections officers at his father's prison don't know what it's like "when you can't tuck your kids in or know that your wife is safe." But one thing he doesn't question is his parents' love or their four-decade-long relationship, which he views as a "blessing," despite the odds.

The youngest of three children, Keshawn and his family participated in visits to the prison. His

Keshawn Green was lucky to have his dad around to teach him how to play basketball—even while his father was incarcerated! Extended visits were vital for Green's childhood development.

mother, Linda, was determined to keep her family together despite the cost. "Between canteen, collect calls, and visiting... I know it's enough to buy a car or a small house," she admits. But they were able to participate in extended visits and so holidays could be kept traditional. "It made the boys feel closer to Charles," Linda recalls. "It wasn't like they didn't know their father—they made memories every visit."

Incredibly, Keshawn's father was able to show him how to pick pecans, hook bait on a fishing pole, and play basketball. The prison grounds boasted a lake and walking trails. The extended visits were instrumental for Keshawn's development. He never felt the strain of making each visit perfect, and he also witnessed the love between his parents play out in a natural and healthy way.

When he was around sixteen, Keshawn elected to cut back on the family house trips, but this was a natural result of his rising confidence as a teen and new feelings of boredom while hanging around his family for a week. He still speaks to his father on the phone and visits him regularly and has even introduced him to his girlfriend. Charles is happy for his son, saying, "I'm not going to choose who he's going to love, but I'll guide him to make smart choices."

Bonding Time

Unlike what you might see on television or Netflix, prisoners aren't always rushing off to the nearest lake for a swim, scheming about how to start an underground, for-profit business, rioting, or being held hostage by former prison guards. A lot of the time, they're feeling alone, isolated, and unproductive despite being in such close confines with other inmates. For these reasons, and others, maintaining family bonds while a parent is incarcerated can be helpful not just to the child but also for the parents themselves. This may not come as a surprise, but children who stay in touch with their parents while they are in prison do not display as many disorderly and anxious behaviors both in and out of the classroom. Additionally, the incarcerated parents have lower recidivism and are more likely to experience a positive reunification with their families upon their release.

While it appears that a high percentage of incarcerated people, mothers especially, keep in touch with family through physical letters and phone calls, these numbers dwindle when it comes to visitations. Of parents who are in state prison, 70 percent report writing letters back and forth with their children, 53 percent talked on the phone, and 42 percent reported that their children had visited in person

Consider picking up a pen and writing a letter to your parent by mail. Families who stay in touch while they're in the prison system are more likely to do well.

since the parent was admitted. Of those in federal prison, mothers were more apt to have had contact, with 84 percent exchanging letters, 85 percent having experienced telephone contact, and 55 percent having had a personal visit.

But for some children, visiting an incarcerated parent would not be productive for their mental or physical health. Some relationships are fraught, some might involve a level of risk for either the parent or child that would not make it worthwhile, and some might involve physical or mental roadblocks that would have to be overcome before a visit would be advisable. That being said, a parent should never be discounted just because he or she is a felon. It is important to keep the children's perspective in mind: to them, these are their parents first and foremost, no matter what. If they want to see them and their parents want them to visit and there are no extenuating circumstances, these are relationships that should not be prevented. But for some, the reasons why they cannot or are not visiting (such as lack of transportation or high costs, unavailability of the child or a caregiver to get them there during visiting hours, lack of visitation privileges on the parent's part, or lack of infrastructure in the prison altogether) should be surmountable. When they aren't, it is heartbreaking.

Who Cares for These Children?

An outsider might believe daily life would generally be very similar for a child whose father is incarcerated versus having a mother in the prison system in the United States, but unfortunately these pictures would more likely look very different. While an incredible 88 percent of incarcerated fathers depend on the mother of their child or children to provide their daily care and a mere 2 percent count on foster care, when the tables are turned only 37 percent of incarcerated women depend on the father. In fact, it is more common for incarcerated mothers to depend on her child or children's grandparents (at 45 percent) than their own partner or the parent of their child. A smaller percentage count on friends or other relatives, while 11 percent of incarcerated women must rely on the foster care system at some point while they are serving time.

While it is sensible to consider who cares for these children while one or more parents is detained, there are some issues that come about from the separation regardless of who is able to step in as primary caregiver. One-quarter of children who reside with a grandparent lives in poverty, while one third lack any kind of health insurance. Likewise, two-thirds of caregivers stepping in for jailed mothers cannot meet the necessary expenses for those children. As a result, these young people find themselves being physically handed around more often from relative to relative or bouncing in and out of foster care as their parents sit in jail. Other resulting issues include separation from siblings (either as a result of well-meaning programs such as Child Welfare and Human Services or to alleviate the responsibility falling entirely on one family member's shoulders) and increased poverty or changes in financial stability while the parent is incarcerated.

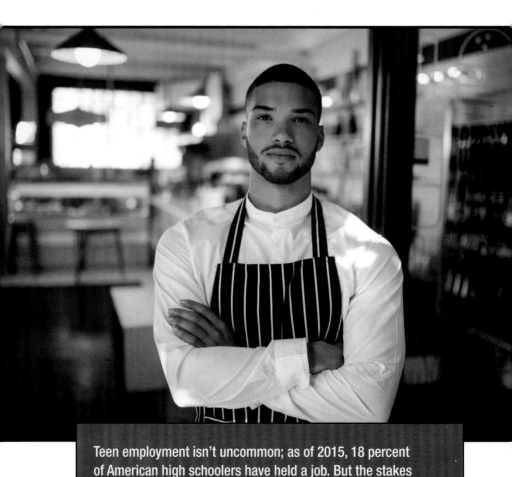

Teen employment isn't uncommon; as of 2015, 18 percent of American high schoolers have held a job. But the stakes increase when you're working to survive, not for pocket money.

As was also expressed earlier, older siblings may also find themselves in unfair positions as caregivers to their younger siblings, while the other parent or primary caregiver is at work—or worse, as sole caregivers, if they are abandoned by other family members altogether. In this case, they may find themselves with daunting responsibilities for any teen, including having to get a job, obtain physical or mental health care for themselves and siblings, and navigate systems designed for adults—all while under pressure to avoid attention from Child Welfare or Human Services and living with the fear that they might be separated from their siblings or taken away from familiar surroundings and an insurmountable amount of stress.

Do You Know Where Your Parents Are?

At the other end of the spectrum, a number of individuals living in America today do not have any idea that one or both of their parents are incarcerated. A study conducted through the Urban Institute Justice Policy Center revealed that one quarter of the children of female prisoners are unaware that their mothers are incarcerated. In these cases, children are most often told that their parent is out of town, in school, or away taking care of ill family members, among other untruths. Sometimes, another caregiver, such as a grandparent or an aunt, uncle, or older cousin, is even named as the false "parent," rather than acknowledging who the real parent is and where they are.

These tactics of avoidance, manipulation of the truth, and outright lying to a child in order to protect them are not healthy. If anything, they are more likely to result in grief when the truth is told or uncovered. What has been done for protection can lead to confusion, worry, uncertainty, fear, and added shame if the child interprets that it was too humiliating for the caregiver to simply share the truth with them from the start. These emotions, mixed with new feelings of distrust for both caregiver and parent, are an unnecessary burden on the child that could have been avoided through truth and open communication.

It is impossible to accept that while one in two American children will have experienced a parent engaging with the criminal system in some way, we are still living in a society in which it is ever acceptable to lie to a child about their parent's whereabouts or who their parents are. Every family has its own reasons for doing the things that they do and making the choices they make—and in these circumstances, it is easy to imagine this coming from a place of love—but consideration must be made for all of the alternatives and the repercussions before this should ever be considered a viable option.

So, how do you tell a child (or a sibling, or even a friend) that their parent is going to prison or is already incarcerated? Be as open and honest with them as you can be, as early on in the process as possible. Children are sensitive to what is going on around them and have probably already sensed that something has changed. Letting them know why you are stressed or upset can help both of you unburden yourselves of negative feelings. Keep things simple. A simple explanation in plain but kind words will get the message across to them that you can be trusted to tell the truth and look after them. Be prepared for questions. Stay open minded and let them ask—and don't just try to give them an easy fix in response. Recognize that the process will not end there, and the child will likely be coping with and questioning the situation for weeks and months to come.

CHAPTER FOUR

Dealing with the Issue in Society

Perhaps at this point you have started to rebuild a healthy relationship with your incarcerated parent. Perhaps your family is doing well at communicating with one another, and you have settled into a routine of phone calls, letters, and visits. Perhaps your approach doesn't look quite like this, but you're all content and, yes, coping. You may not quite feel happy about it, but you can feel yourself coming to terms with it. Or, maybe you have come to terms with it.

And then one day, you turn on the television and a popular talk show host is telling his or her audience that more "bad" people should be incarcerated or that rehabilitation of prisoners doesn't work because they are already set up to fail, and your little machine begins to break down—one of the cogs stops turning or a spring gets loose—and you find yourself feeling angry or sad or incredibly lonely. You thought you'd gotten past this phase. So what happened?

What Is Advocacy?

Coping is an ongoing state of being. It requires work and maintenance to stay healthy, both mentally and physically. Internal stressors are hardly the only causes. External factors can also affect a person's health and well-being. For some, coping includes getting involved with sports, volunteering, or doing community service. But for others, coping looks like advocacy. One major way to deal with everything you are experiencing is to channel your negative emotions into positive change.

Child Trends calls for policymakers and lawmakers to increase funding and programs intended to decrease children's distress and humiliation, enhance contact between incarcerated parents and their children, and allow for more child-friendly jail time visits with the parent. In 2015, the Federal Communications Commission (FCC) slashed the cost of prison phone calls in the United States, setting a new price cap of $1.65 for fifteen minutes of call time. In this case, a major nonprofit research center made a suggestion, and the national government followed through on it. The effects of this price cap are still being assessed. But without advocacy, or public support for or recommendation of a particular cause or policy, this change may never have occurred.

Some women's prisons have begun to introduce special visitation programs in response to studies, trends, and advocates. These programs, which allow children to bond with their parents in prison without strict security procedures, should be extended to fathers, argues David Murphey of Child Trends. These extended visits—which have previously only enjoyed state by state funding (and so, limited access) and have been disappearing in the past two decades because of overcrowding and underfunding—have proved to be one of the best ways to strengthen bonds between children and parents and make sure they will be maintained. With the voice of advocacy, particularly from teens, there is a greater chance now than ever that voices like Murphey's will be heard and heeded.

Advocates have also called for a "two-generation approach" to address issues stemming from the possession of a criminal record and the barriers to opportunity that may cause. It is detrimental, in fact, to ignore the intergenerational consequences of incarceration, and by involving the needs of both the child and the parent in the same system or approach, the chances for both generations to succeed get higher while the overall rate of recidivism is lowered. This two-generation approach, as it applies to the prison

Vending machines are a visiting room fixture, but what's inside them tends to be monotonous. Healthier, more varied choices can help lead to more vibrant visiting hours.

system, could be as simple as finding a common focus for parents and children. For example, stocking healthier foods in the vending machines while also providing group sessions about nutrition for parents would both improve the atmosphere in the visitors' center for children and help parents feel more prepared and capable of caring for their children upon reentry.

Cadence

Visiting conditions in prison are always uncomfortable. Between the hard seats, limited face time, and rules regarding touching, the hour you get to spend with a parent may not be ideal. Add to that long wait times, crowded visiting rooms, and the procedure of being frisked and searched just to get in, and the sacrifice of going may hardly seem worth it. For some families, it's not. Money presents as an obstacle before even arriving at the prison, as families in poverty can struggle to get time off work and find the means to get there (particularly without a car) and debate whether to bring young children along, find childcare, or leave some family members home unattended. Prisoners are also moved within the system, sometimes without warning, only telling family after the transfer process is complete.

The longer the visit, the better the connection for the child. Ann Adalist-Estrin, director of the National Resource Center on Children and Families of the Incarcerated at Rutgers University, has assessed this through a process called "cadence," a series of group developmental stages labeled form, storm, norm, and perform. These stages refer to the type of conversation and bonding in which the child (and parent) is engaged. Initially, it is easy for

It can take time to get reacquainted with an incarcerated parent when you're not used to one another. Longer visiting hours allow for richer experiences, as families become more comfortable together.

the child to "form" a relationship with the parent—they are delighted to see one other. During a longer visit, though, parents and children may feel more comfortable moving into difficult topics involving emotions such as sadness and anger ("storm") because they are confident they will have the time to resolve them and return to normal before they are separated. However, in a short visit, children tend to stay in the safe zone, waffling between "form" and "norm" because they are uncomfortable and worried that they won't have time to resolve anything deeper. This keeps conversations on the surface, leaving parents and children yearning for more.

Public and Private Support

In the past twenty years, a public and private support system has developed in lieu of a direct form of federal funding and support for children with parents in prison. Some states have set up programs themselves, while others, such as Mississippi, have no state-funded programs at all, only nonprofit efforts focused on parental incarceration.

Oregon's State Department of Corrections oversees the Children of Incarcerated Parents Project, which involves Head Start programs, mental health services, and educational opportunities and has been in operation for over a decade. Head Start is a valuable tool for low-income children and their families that provides comprehensive early childhood education, health, nutrition, and parent involvement services and is designed to enhance the child's physical and emotional well-being and cognitive skills in the formative and transitional period between preschool and elementary school. Head Start is always looking for young volunteers and can be a great way to get involved with and serve your own community as a teenager.

In 2013, the White House created Children of Incarcerated Parents, a Federal Interagency Working Group that brings agencies across the government together to evaluate federal programs and policies affecting this demographic. Their main aims are to

Volunteering with programs like Head Start is a great way to give your own time and knowledge back to the community, while making use of your own experiences.

offer service providers the educational and technical support they need, to better explain and upgrade public policy, and to increase public awareness of the challenges facing children of incarcerated parents. Sadly, when the Justice Department was awarded $53 million in 2015 for grants, only three (worth $1.2 million) were dedicated to programs explicitly for children: counseling, mentoring, and, in one single case, visitation.

The Annie E. Casey Foundation has built resources and organizations designed to "preserve the parent-child connection," including literacy programs, mentoring and counseling for children, and parent-child visiting programs. With a number of partnerships in the public, private, and community spheres, this foundation is massive and covers much more territory than just the issues engaged with here. Some of their initiatives cover all fifty states, as well as Washington, DC, Puerto Rico, and the US Virgin Islands. They are involved with a number of on-the-ground strategies, including the Kids Count Network, the Center for Working Families, and Reducing Youth Incarceration. They have also published numerous reports with a focus on children with incarcerated parents, overviewing the literature, documenting recent progress in the area, and exploring prospects for future development. They have also published a primer on the subject for social workers.

Both children and young adults can benefit from having a mentor in their lives, someone they can look up to—whether literally or maybe just metaphorically.

A Feeling of Hope

Hope House in Washington, DC, founded in 1998, is a nonprofit focused on helping parents stay connected with their children through programs that include summer camp as well as recorded books. Activist and Hope House executive director Carol Fennelly believes in the power of educational awareness programs created as a means to remove or alleviate children's embarrassment and stigma. She knows it can be hard to face judgment from teachers, peers, and other community members. "Sometimes people aren't even aware that they react negatively once they first learn that a student has a parent behind bars," Fennelly points out, going on to say, "But that child certainly can hear it and feel it."

Fennelly has been running a week-long program called Camp Hope through Hope House for sixteen years, in which a small group of children—nearly all

Because of Carol Fennelly and her Hope House initiative, young people like these two sisters are able to keep in touch with their incarcerated fathers. Here, they connect via videoconferencing.

from Baltimore—are invited down to the Federal Correctional Institution in Cumberland, Maryland, where each of their fathers are in prison. Some have not seen their fathers in years, and others speak on the phone fairly regularly. This experience—an entire week of daytime visits in which the fathers and children participate in activities together—seems to be wholly new for all of them. Fennelly finds that after the week is over, the children are more relaxed, and their grades improve at school. She knows the connection is temporary, but firmly believes the effects are positive and lasting for both parent and child. Beyond the Maryland-based camp, she runs a similar setup in North Carolina and has been contacted by prisons in California and Texas that are keen to adopt it themselves.

Nationally, there aren't many similar programs in place; most of the government-funded extended visit programs were cut for budgetary reasons over the past several decades, and the most comparable program today is Girl Scouts Beyond Bars. Ebony Ruhland, research associate for the Robina Institute of Criminal Law and Criminal Justice, summarizes the benefits of programs like these: "For the first time, kids create a network of friends with incarcerated parents; father and child can bond, which gives the father a feeling of responsibility after he's released; and the child benefits because kids miss having that attachment to their parent."

Getting Involved

But how can teenagers really get involved with advocacy themselves? So many of these programs are open to engaging with young people, either as volunteers and program participants or as consultants. You can work with some organizations on their planning committees and boards; if there is a specific organization you want to work with, check their website for their preferred method of contact and get in touch with them. You may find they already have something for you to do; if not, suggest that they start to include youth with incarcerated parents on their planning committees and boards. If you are requesting a particular change in a policy or procedure that has an effect on you, make sure to develop your thoughts into a well-formed idea before approaching them. Even if you are going in for a meeting or having a phone conversation, practice what you're going to say before you say it. If you are writing to them, get a teacher, parent, or friend you trust to look over the draft first.

Once you have your foot in the door, you can start to become a part of the efforts to design and develop visiting and mentor programs. Don't forget to campaign for financial support and funding when appropriate for the most powerful programming. Think about what you would want as a child growing up with an incarcerated parent in the United States, and use your new platform to advocate for that. Where were the holes in your own support network? Recall the five pillars of family well-being: income, savings and assets, education, housing, family strength, and stability. Does this program focus on any of those elements in their policies for change? Remember the issues that you and your family members or friends faced (and maybe still do), and channel your efforts into those topics. Some common topics include mental health, social behavior, educational outlook, emotional suffering, practical difficulties, disrupted family life, social stigma, financial hardship (because of loss of a parent's income), loss of parental rights (because of length of time in the foster care system), child support, and the list could go on! How could the organization you're advocating for be better at one of these things (or something altogether individual to your personal experience)?

10 Great Questions to Ask a Mentor

1. What are some activities my parent and I can do together during our next contact visit?

2. Are there any local programs set up where I can meet other teens like me who also have a parent in prison?

3. My nonincarcerated parent (or guardian) is always busy. What are some ways I can help or show my appreciation for all he or she does for me (and my siblings)?

4. I want to set up a club at school to raise awareness about the prison system and being the child of an incarcerated person. Whom should I talk to?

5. Sometimes I worry that if I open up to my parents too much it will be a burden on them or that they just don't have time for me. Is there anyone else I can talk to about my feelings?

6. I find myself getting bored when I sit down to write a letter to my parent, but I know it's really important to him or her. Do you have any advice for me on finding more stimulating topics that would interest both of us?

(continued on the next page)

(continued from the previous page)

7. There aren't many things for children to do while they're visiting the prison. Who can I talk to about fixing things up in the visitors' room?

8. What are some things I can do from home to help my incarcerated parent between visits?

9. I think I'm ready to talk to my friends about my parent being in prison. How do I start?

10. Thinking about my situation makes me feel frustrated. What can I do when I want to just sit and be sad?

Healing from Trauma

According to the PEW Charitable Trusts, the typical amount of time federal inmates have served has increased dramatically between 1988 and 2012—spiking from 17.9 to 37.5 months, with significant increases across all main federal crime classes (violent, property, drug, public order, weapon, and immigration offenses). For drug offenders, accounting for about 50 percent of the federal prison population, the amount of time served jumped from fewer than two years to almost five. Research shows that longer prison terms do not have much of an effect as a crime prevention strategy but that lengthier sentences are more detrimental for families involved in the system for a variety of reasons. With so many parents incarcerated today, why is sentence length still going up across the board?

One can only suspect that part of this has to do with rising fear on the side of the public and scaremongering on the side of the prosecution and the judiciary system at large. In an attempt to make our streets "safer," more and more Americans were placed behind bars. But the reality remains: whether eighteen months or three years, those offenders are coming out. Except for a relatively small number of people who face a death sentence or a life sentence, all inmates who survive prison will eventually be released, and many of them will be coming home to their families.

A Positive Reunion

Though the thought of having your parent back in your life after he or she has been away most likely sounds thrilling to you, for many teens this excitement is laced with a level of doubt, hesitancy, and even fear. What if your father or mother does not fit neatly back into the domestic dynamic you had built together before he or she was in prison? What if he or she (or you!) has changed while he or she was away, and things aren't the same anymore? What if he or she struggles to find a job or readjusting proves to be too hard? Or, what if your parents have split up while they were apart and now your mother or father won't be returning to the house? It's easy for all of these questions and scenarios to spring up in your imagination, but try to be realistic.

Reuniting with your parent will be momentous—but it may also feel confusing, overwhelming, or even frightening. Allow time to adjust and get to know each other in this context again.

The bottom line is that no matter what, things are going to be different. It is better to adjust to that reality and accept it now before your parent arrives home, so you can work on making your relationship going forward a positive one once he or she does.

Of course, for some families, the parent won't be able to return to his or her child's primary home. Perhaps he or she wasn't living there to begin with. Perhaps he or she may pose an amount of danger to the family now, because of the nature of the crime. If your parent harmed someone—especially you or another family member—reuniting the family will be a tentative process most likely involving a counselor or another professional. Whatever emotions you are feeling, positive or negative, it is important for you to recognize them as valid and find ways of expressing them—to a friend, a guidance counselor, a teacher, a mentor, or another trusted adult. Also, remember that they are likely to change and to remain in flux for quite some time. The "reunion" phase will not be over quickly and could take years to fully resolve.

It is just as important for you to know it's not your job to make everything better for your family or to always keep things positive and upbeat. You may feel concerned about bonding properly with your parent, but your parent is just as accountable for his or her actions as you feel you are. Your mother or father has to earn back both your trust and respect again, and you'll need to be able to lean on him or her for support. In fact, testing whether or not you can lean on your parent may bring you a step toward regaining that trust. Both you and your parents should keep in mind, though, that your expectations of one another may not be met immediately when you reunite. Despite phone calls updating her along the way, your parent may still see you as the child she left behind when she was first incarcerated, and vice versa. It may be easier to picture your parent as he was or as a version of your dad that you built up while your parent was away. Both of you will need to take a few steps backward to gain some clarity. Pause and reassess. Who do you see in front of you now? And what is it fair to say your parent sees in you? Try to honor the versions of each other that exist in the now, rather than clinging to the past or some unrealized iteration.

The Importance of Support

A large part of healing, whether it's of the mental or physical sort, is reliant on having a recognizable support system. If someone you knew was diagnosed with cancer, you wouldn't expect him or her to be tossed out of the community and told to get on with the healing process by himself or herself. Likely, that person would be embraced more fully by the community than before. Casseroles might start appearing on his or her doorstep. Neighbors might offer rides to the clinic for treatment. If nothing else, neighbors would ask how the person was doing. Whether they chose to lean on it or not, the person would have the full sympathy of the community.

Unfortunately, not all traumas are considered equal in society; though it would be hard to see the death of a classmate's parent as anything but a tragedy, some might not treat the incarceration of a parent as being on the same spectrum of loss. It is this fear of being taunted at school that may prevent someone with a parent in prison from making connections with classmates or peers. For example, young prison activist Xacey Willis may fight for civil rights on the weekend, but at school she keeps her father's incarceration a secret. Despite having a cousin in the same class whose father is also in prison, she reveals, "I just tell them that he [sic] at work." She's not ashamed, just trying to avoid the taunts.

Despite these challenges, it is important to seek out a support system of your own. When a person finds another person who shares his or her story, it can be a point of bonding. Two people (or more) finding out they each have a parent in prison can give them an instant sense of connection that, over time, can build into a larger community in and of itself. It is important to remember that at a person's core, he or she largely wants the same things: to be loved, supported, and successful and to have friends. This desire is not

Create a support system. Having people in your life with whom you share aspects of your story and who are open to hearing and accepting you without judgment can be very rewarding.

unique to children of incarcerated parents, or even teenagers, but the human race. Some ways to do this are by asking for help, joining a support group—either online or in person—and joining local programs in your community tailored to the specific services you need (such as transportation during visiting hours, mentoring, or help with classwork). Keep in mind that if you're not able to find or create an appropriate support group in your own town or community, you can find help and support online in a variety of places. Project WHAT! (based in Oakland, California) and Girl Scouts Beyond Bars are both worthwhile places to start when searching for additional information. You can also check out resource suggestions on government websites or websites linked to other organizations.

Sesame Street

In 2013, Sesame Workshop launched a character named Alex whose father is incarcerated for an initiative called Little Children, Big Challenges: Incarceration. Alex is featured in a bilingual tool kit that's been distributed through a number of nonprofit organizations, including criminal justice groups,

Sesame Street is known for uniting entertainment and education, and the character of Alex is no exception. Exclusive to the Little Children, Big Challenges initiative, Alex's father is incarcerated.

social workers, after-school programs, and state corrections departments. Sesame Workshop has been known to distribute free multimedia resources for families learning to cope with a variety of situations; in a different kit, for example, they created resources for families with parents deployed overseas.

Alex's kit includes videos, a mobile app, and a storybook geared toward young children, as well as materials for caregivers. It has been distributed in physical form across ten states to government agencies, nongovernmental organizations (NGOs), schools, and other groups that specialize in helping

(continued on the next page)

(contined from the previous page)

incarcerated people and their families. It has also gone out in a newsletter to more than 7.7 million partners of the program, the free app has been downloaded thousands of times, and in the first two months alone its home page had eighty-five thousand views. If you live in one of these states or have younger siblings with access to an app-friendly device, perhaps you have even seen Alex for yourself. But despite the hype, Alex has been labeled as unlikely to appear on the TV show. "It's just not the best way to reach the specific intended audience," says Lynn Chwatsky, the vice president for initiatives, partnerships, and community engagement at Sesame Workshop.

Chwatsky acknowledges these children "may feel ashamed or abandoned or angry about their incarcerated parent," which is often escalated by trauma from classmates and peers who find out. So why, if it's intended "as a way to help children cope with the emotions that come from a situation they may be too young to fully grasp," wouldn't the specific audience include bullies and everyday students who have added to these shameful feelings? Televising Alex would normalize this Muppet's story—and, in turn, deter more children from acting out against their peers, turning bullies into friends.

Giving Yourself Permission

You've come a long way at this point toward coping. You've picked up that pen and written out your feelings. Or maybe you've started going for runs to clear your mind. You've stopped feeling angry and frustrated all the time. Perhaps you've joined an art class or a soccer team or an after-school club. You've started volunteering. You've talked to your parent in prison and your family outside of prison, and you've started consciously helping out around the house more often. You've told your friends about your last contact visit and shared how it made you feel. Maybe you've spoken to younger members of your community who have parents in prison and have helped a few of them with homework, advice about what to talk to their parents about on the phone, or what to say to their families when they're feeling upset. You've even written a few letters to local and national groups offering your advice from the perspective of someone with an incarcerated parent. Or possibly you've stood up to classmates and started a group at school. You've seen a guidance counselor. (You probably haven't done all of these things, but hopefully you've considered a few!) You should be feeling validated, important, and affirmed. It's time to sit back and feel proud of your accomplishments. You are a person who matters, and

One rewarding way to cope with negative emotions is by making (or continuing) a running routine; getting exercise and fresh air are both great ways to combat stress.

your parent is incarcerated and that matters, too. But wait, that's not how you feel?

Sometimes the hardest person to convince is you. That's why it's so important to give yourself permission. It's OK to be the child of an incarcerated parent. It's OK to have a parent in jail. You are not going to end up in prison just because you have a family member in the system. Your life is your own, and there is no shame in it. Classmates may have bullied and harassed you and people might make judgmental comments, but you got through it and you will continue to get through it. You are an individual who is growing and learning and changing every day. In an article for the *Nation*, Sylvia A. Harvey writes, "No one ever gave me permission to wear this uncomfortable truth." Here is your permission. You don't need to stay quiet.

You are a witness of something that has become statistically commonplace in America, yet remains swept under the rug. You have borne something inside yourself, potentially on your own,

What are your ambitions? As you adjust to the changes in your life, the time will come to reassess your goals and continue on your path to achieving them.

that no one today should be carrying around in secret. You aren't a victim; you're one of the enlightened. There is no shame in being enlightened. So, take your insight and go forth with it. Carry it inside of you and be the person you want to be, not the person anyone else tells you that you are. Now you are coping.

Moving on Without Forgetting

Moving on from trauma doesn't mean forgetting what happened. Once you have begun to process or come to terms with your own personal situation, you will be able to start considering it as just one element of your larger self or even as a part of your past altogether. Suddenly, all the time you spent thinking about these issues in your head without knowing how to deal with them can be spent elsewhere. You might even find that you can use some of the energy you'd been spending on dealing with these issues on other parts of your life.

Not everything is going to be solved right away. If your parent is still incarcerated, even if you are better equipped to deal with that element of your life, it is still a part of it. If you missed your parent before, you are probably still going to miss him or her now. Because of the nature of the system, with strict biweekly or monthly visitation times and fees for phone privileges, your parent will most likely still miss out on some big events and certainly some everyday opportunities to be a part of your life. The difference now is that you have the tools to manage your feelings in healthy ways when these situations arise and you have the habits in place to recover from them more quickly and easily.

Just remember that your friends and family members outside of prison are there for you, and you do not need to take any of this on by yourself. You are not alone. In fact, you may even want to take this knowledge and spread it around in your community. Remember how it felt to be a child with a parent in prison and consider reaching out to other younger children in your own community. Be a mentor. The best way to spread positive change is by reaching out a hand to someone in need. If you are able to do that, then you'll know you've made it.

Glossary

adverse Against one's interests; negative or harmful.

advocacy Public support for or recommendation of a particular cause or policy.

altercation A heated and angry dispute.

anxiety A medical term used to describe an overwhelming sense of doubt and fear marked by physical signs.

dependency A state of being reliant on something else.

destitute Lacking to the point of extreme poverty.

external Concerned with what is outside of a person's body.

incarcerated To be put in prison.

infrastructure The basic resources of a system or organization.

intergenerational Concerning multiple groups of people, where each group individually has been born around the same time.

internal Concerned with what is inside of a person's mind.

intervention To interfere with the course of something, especially a condition or process, for a positive change.

mitigate To make less severe; alleviate.

premature Happening or arriving before the proper, intended time.

reactive Occurring as a result of a stimulus, such as stress or emotional upset.

recidivism A relapse into a previous condition, particularly criminal behavior.

regression Shifting toward a less mature state, as an earlier mental or behavioral level.

socioeconomic Involving a combination of social and economic factors.

status quo The way things are; normalcy.

termination Ending or ceasing to exist; the act of being finished.

trauma A disordered mental or physical state resulting from severe emotional stress or physical injury.

Canadian Families and Corrections Network (CFCN)

Box 35040

Kingston, ON K7L 5S5

Canada

(888) 371-2326

Website: http://www.cfcn-rcafd.org

Facebook: @cfcn.rcafd

Twitter: @CFCN_RCAFD

CFCN is building stronger and safer communities by assisting families affected by criminal behavior, incarceration, and community reintegration. The organization is dedicated to providing practical information, support, and advice for those that have a loved one involved in the justice system.

Fostering, Empowering, Advocating Together (FEAT) for Children of Incarcerated Parents

432 Horner Avenue

Etobicoke, ON M8W 2B3

Canada

(416) 505-5333

Website: http://featforchildren.org

Facebook: @FEAT-for-Children-of-Incarcerated -Parents

Twitter: @FEATforchildren

FEAT for Children of Incarcerated Parents was founded in 2011 to support the needs of the over fifty thousand children in Ontario that have a parent in the criminal justice system.

Girl Scouts Beyond Bars (GSBB)

9620 SW Barbur Boulevard

Portland, OR 97219

(503) 977-6815

Website: http://www.girlscoutsosw.org/en/about -girl-scouts/our-program/ways-to-participate /gsbb.html

Facebook and Twitter: @GirlScoutsOSW

Instagram: @girlscoutsosw

Girl Scouts Beyond Bars serves girls whose mothers are incarcerated at Coffee Creek Correctional Facility in Wilsonville, Oregon. GSBB's primary goal is to lessen the effect of parent-child separation.

Office of Juvenile Justice and Delinquency Prevention (OJJDP)

810 Seventh Street NW

Washington, DC 20531

(202) 307-5911

Website: https://www.ojjdp.gov

The OJJDP collaborates with professionals from diverse disciplines to improve juvenile justice policies and practices. It aims to help juveniles in crisis by supporting states, local communities, and tribal jurisdictions in their efforts to develop and implement effective programs for juveniles.

Parenting Inside Out

(503) 351-0164

Website: http://www.parentinginsideout.org

Facebook: @Parenting-Inside-Out

Twitter: @PrntngInsideOut

Parenting Inside Out is an evidence-based, cognitive-behavioral skills training program that assists mothers and fathers who are parenting from prison. The program is listed in the National Registry of Evidence-based Programs and Practices of the HHS, Substance Abuse and Mental Health Services Administration.

Project WHAT!

110 Broadway

Oakland, CA 94607

(510) 268-8116

Website: http://communityworkswest.org/program
  /project-what

Facebook: @communityworkswest

Twitter: @communityworksw

Project WHAT! strives to create a community that
  allows young people with parents behind bars to
  use their voice, pride, and power and supports
  them in creating policy change that reflects the
  needs of youth and families with an incarcerated
  loved one.

US Dream Academy

5950 Symphony Woods Road, Suite 504

Columbia, MD 21044

(410) 772-7143

Website: http://www.usdreamacademy.org

Facebook: @USDreamAcademy

Twitter: @US_DreamAcademy

The US Dream Academy provides after-school
  and mentoring programs for at-risk youth,
  especially those with incarcerated parents, in
  eight communities across the United States.

Birtha, Becky, and Maja Kastelic. *Far Apart, Close in Heart: Being a Family When a Loved One Is Incarcerated.* Chicago, IL: Albert Whitman & Company, 2017.

Brodak, Molly. *Bandit: A Daughter's Memoir.* New York, NY: Black Cat, 2016.

Cook, Julia, and Anita DuFalla. *What Do I Say About That? Coping with an Incarcerated Parent.* Chattanooga, TN: National Center for Youth Issues, 2015.

Frakes, C. *Prison Island: A Graphic Memoir.* San Francisco, CA: Zest Books, 2015.

Goulbourne, Jean. *Janice.* London, UK: HopeRoad, 2014.

Hinton, Kerry. *Incarceration in America* (In the News). New York, NY: Rosen Publishing, 2010.

Poole, Hilary W. *Incarceration and Families.* Broomall, PA: Mason Crest, 2017.

Shofner, Corabel. *Almost Paradise.* New York, NY: Farrar, Straus and Giroux, 2017.

Wittbold, Maureen. *Let's Talk About When Your Parent Is in Jail.* New York, NY: Rosen Publishing, 1997.

Young, Judy. *Promise.* Ann Arbor, MI: Sleeping Bear Press, 2016.

Bibliography

Alexander, Amy. "Why Children with Parents in Prison Are Especially Burdened." *Atlantic*, December 14, 2015. https://www.theatlantic .com/politics/archive/2015/12/why-children -with-parents-in-prison-are-especially -burdened/433638.

Children's Bureau. "Child Welfare Practice with Families Affected by Parental Incarceration." Child Welfare Information Gateway, October 2015. https://www.childwelfare.gov/pubPDFs /parental_incarceration.pdf.

Christian, Steve. "Children of Incarcerated Parents." National Conference of State Legislatures, March 2009. http://www.ncsl.org/documents /cyf/childrenofincarceratedparents.pdf.

CSG Justice Center Staff. "Bill to Reauthorize Second Chance Act Introduced in U.S. House of Representatives." Council of State Governments, June 13, 2017. https://csgjusticecenter.org /jc/bill-to-reauthorize-second-chance-act -introduced-in-u-s-house-of-representatives.

Eisen, Lauren-Brooke, and Inimai Chettiar. "39% of Prisoners Should Not Be in Prison." *Time*, December 9, 2016. http://time.com/4596081 /incarceration-report.

Glaze, Lauren E., and Laura M. Maruschak. "Parents in Prison and Their Minor Children." Bureau of

Justice Statistics, March 30, 2010. https://www
.bjs.gov/content/pub/pdf/pptmc.pdf.

Harris, Amanda. "Supporting Your Child
When a Parent Is in Jail." Trauma and Grief
Network, October 2014. https://tgn.anu.edu
.au/wp-content/uploads/2014/10/Supporting
-your-child-when-a-parent-is-in-jail_0.pdf.

Harvey, Sylvia A. "2.7 Million Kids Have Parents
in Prison. They're Losing Their Right to Visit."
Nation, December 2, 2015. https://www
.thenation.com/article/2-7m-kids-have-parents
-in-prison-theyre-losing-their-right-to-visit.

Jenkins, Nash. "1 in 14 U.S. Children Has Had
a Parent in Prison, Says New Study." *Time*,
October 27, 2015. http://time.com/4088385
/child-trends-incarceration-study.

Kristof, Nicholas. "Mothers in Prison." *New
York Times*, November 25, 2016. https://www
.nytimes.com/2016/11/25/opinion/sunday
/mothers-in-prison.html.

La Vigne, Nancy G., Elizabeth Davies, and Diana
Brazzell. "Broken Bonds: Understanding
and Addressing the Needs of Children
with Incarcerated Parents." Urban Institute
Justice Policy Center, February 2008.
https://www.urban.org/sites/default/files
/publication/31486/411616-Broken-Bonds
-Understanding-and-Addressing-the-Needs

-of-Children-with-Incarcerated-Parents.pdf.

Leber, Jessica. "Meet Alex The Muppet, The First Sesame Street Character with a Father in Jail." *Fast Company*, September 18, 2013. https:// www.fastcompany.com/3017556/meet-alex -the-muppet-the-first-sesame-street-character -with-a-father-in-jail.

Miller, Keva M. "The Impact of Parental Incarceration on Children: An Emerging Need for Effective Interventions." *Child and Adolescent Social Work Journal*, August 31, 2006. https:// link.springer.com/article/10.1007/s10560-006 -0065-6.

Murphey, David, and P. Mae Cooper. "Behind Bars: What Happens to Their Children?" Child Trends, October 2015. https://www.childtrends .org/wp-content/uploads/2015/10/2015 -42ParentsBehindBars.pdf.

Oates, Tom, Madeline Solan, and Alix McLearen. "Working with the Correctional System and Incarcerated Parents." Child Welfare Information Gateway Podcast, Retrieved October 10, 2017. https://www.acf.hhs.gov/sites/default/files/cb /cw_podcast_incarcerated_parents_transcript .pdf.

Office of Public Affairs. "The Children of Incarcerated Parents Project." Oregon Department of Corrections, 2003. http://www.oregon.gov/doc /OC/docs/oam/2003_childrens_project.pdf.

Paquette, Danielle. "One in Nine Black Children Has Had a Parent in Prison." *Washington Times*, October 27, 2015. https://www.washingtonpost .com/news/wonk/wp/2015/10/27/one-in -nine-black-children-have-had-a-parent-in -prison/?utm_term=.3d88a300cc7c.

Peterson, Bryce, Jocelyn Fontaine, Emma Kurs, and Lindsey Cramer. "Children of Incarcerated Parents Framework Document: Promising Practices, Challenges, and Recommendations for the Field." Urban Institute, June 2015. https://www.urban.org /sites/default/files/publication/53721/2000256 -Children-of-Incarcerated-Parents-Framework -Document.pdf.

Phippen, J. Weston. "What Happens When 12 Kids Spend a Week in Prison with Their Fathers." *Atlantic*, October 27, 2015. https:// www.theatlantic.com/politics/archive/2015/10 /what-happens-when-12-kids-spend-a-week -in-prison-with-their-fathers/433221.

Prison Fellowship. "FAQs About Children of Prisoners." Prison Fellowship. Retrieved August 25, 2017. https://www.prisonfellowship.org /resources/training-resources/family/ministry -basics/faqs-about-children-of-prisoners.

Public Safety Performance Packet. "Prison Time Surges for Federal Inmates." PEW Charitable Trusts, November 18, 2015. http://www .pewtrusts.org/en/research-and-analysis/issue

-briefs/2015/11/prison-time-surges-for-federal-inmates.

Rascoe, Ayesha. "Obama Administration Revamps Child Support Rules for Prisoners." Reuters, December 20, 2016. https://www.reuters.com /article/us-usa-criminaljustice-childsupport /obama-administration-revamps-child -support-rules-for-prisoners-idUSKBN1482IK.

Reilly, Katie. "Sesame Street Reaches Out to 2.7 Million American Children with an Incarcerated Parent." Pew Research Center, June 21, 2013. http://www.pewresearch.org /fact-tank/2013/06/21/sesame-street-reaches -out-to-2-7-million-american-children-with -an-incarcerated-parent.

Ruiz, Dorothy Smith, and Albert Kopak. "The Consequences of Parental Incarceration for African American Mothers, Children, and Grandparent Caregivers." *Journal of Pan African Studies*, November 2014. http://www .jpanafrican.org/docs/vol7no6/7.6-4-Ruitz -Oct26.pdf.

Social Work Policy Institute. "Children with Incarcerated Parents." Social Work Policy Institute, June 21, 2008. http://www .socialworkpolicy.org/research/children-with -incarcerated-parents.html.

Travis, Jeremy, Elizabeth McBride, and Amy Solomon. "Families Left Behind: The Hidden Costs of Incarceration and Reentry." Urban Institute Justice Policy Center, June 2005. https://www.urban.org/sites/default/files /publication/50461/310882-Families-Left -Behind.pdf.

Vallas, Rebecca, Melissa Boteach, Rachel West, and Jackie Odum. "Removing Barriers to Opportunity for Parents with Criminal Records and Their Children." Center for American Progress, December 10, 2015. https://www.americanprogress.org/issues/ poverty/reports/2015/12/10/126902/ removing-barriers-to-opportunity-for parents-with-criminal-records-and-their -children.

Wagner, Peter, and Bernadette Rabuy. "Mass Incarceration: The Whole Pie 2017." Prison Policy Initiative, March 14, 2017. https://www .prisonpolicy.org/reports/pie2017.html.

YOUTH.gov. "Tip Sheet for Youth: Youth Supporting Fellow Youth Who Have an Incarcerated Parent." YOUTH.gov, June 2016. https://youth.gov/sites/default/files/COIP _TipSheet_Youth_Final.pdf.

Index

About the Author

Carolyn DeCarlo is a poet and fiction writer from Baltimore, Maryland, who now lives in New Zealand. She has worked as a teacher in jail and prison and in St. Elizabeth's Hospital in Washington, DC. She was also a mentor for the ASK Program, serving at-risk youth in the juvenile justice system of Washington, DC, and has volunteered for 826DC. She has a BA in English and psychology from Georgetown University, where she also studied forensics, and an MFA in creative writing from the University of Maryland, College Park. She has written several chapbooks, including *Green Place* (Enjoy Journal, 2015).

About the Expert

Heather Gay, LCSW, has been practicing in the field of social work and nonprofit work for more than fifteen years. Hay received her master's in social work from New York University in 2007. She has experience providing direct clinical psychotherapy through an outpatient mental health clinic in Brooklyn. She has worked at the Ali Forney Center since 2008, providing services to LGBTQ youth, ages sixteen to twenty-four, who are experiencing homelessness. Gay began at Ali Forney as a mental health specialist, providing direct-care mental health services. Currently, she is the deputy executive director of programs, overseeing all mental health, drop-in, and housing program services. Additionally, Gay completed a two-year psychotherapy training program at the Institute for Contemporary Psychotherapy and currently has a small psychotherapy private practice. She is also an adjunct professor at the NYU School of Social Work and previously in the Silberman School of Social Work at Hunter College.

Photo Credits

Cover sirtravelalot/Shutterstock.com; pp. 4–5 Andrew Aitchison/Corbis Historical/Getty Images; p. 9 Robert Nickelsberg/Hulton Archive/Getty Images; p. 10 Hemera Technologies/AbleStock.com/Thinkstock; pp. 12–13 Andrew Aitchison/Corbis News/Getty Images; pp. 18–19 Andy Cross/Denver Post/Getty Images; p. 21 SpeedKingz/Shutterstock.com; p. 24 © iStockphoto.com/kali9; p. 28 Stephen Lovekin/Getty Images; pp. 23–33 tommaso79/Shutterstock.com; p. 39 Saul Loeb/AFP/Getty Images; p. 41 Angelo Merendino/Getty Images; p. 43 martin-dm/E+/Getty Images; p. 46 © iStockphoto.com/KatarzynaBialasiewicz; p. 48 © iStockphoto.com/baona; p. 50 © iStockphoto.com/wundervisuals; p. 52 peepo/E+/Getty Images; p. 55 SolVazquez/iStock/Thinkstock; p. 58 Wavebreakmedia/iStock/Thinkstock; p. 65 Marc DEVILLE/Gamma-Rapho/Getty Images; p. 67 Tim Rue/Corbis Historical/Getty Images; p. 69 Design Pics/Thinkstock; p. 71 Cameron Spencer/Photodisc/Thinkstock; pp. 72–73 The Washington Post/Getty Images; p. 81 shironosov/iStock/Thinkstock; p. 85 Evgenna/iStock/Thinkstock; p. 87 Kris Connor/Getty Images; pp. 90–91 Halfpoint/Shutterstock.com; pp. 92–93 mangostar/Shutterstock.com.

Design and Layout: Nicole Russo-Duca; Editor and Photo Researcher: Heather Moore Niver